The Great War
Display Team

ERNIE HOBLYN

AMBERLEY

Acknowledgements

Firstly I would like to thank the photographers who have allowed me to use their beautiful pictures to illustrate this book; without them it would not have been possible.

Secondly, my thanks to all the members of the Team, both past and present, who have helped me with the Team history and written passages about their own aircraft for inclusion in the book. What better expert can you have than the person who regularly flies a First World War aircraft in mock-combat – apart from one who flew in real combat? There are none of the latter still around now, sadly.

Lastly many thanks to Bruce for finding time in his hectic schedule to write the Foreword for the book. I know few people who are busier than Bruce so I am very grateful to him.

First published 2019

Amberley Publishing
The Hill, Stroud,
Gloucestershire, GL5 4EP

www.amberley-books.com

ISBN 978 1 4456 8593 9 (print)
ISBN 978 1 4456 8594 6 (ebook)

British Library Cataloguing in Publication Data.
A catalogue record for this book is available from the British Library.

Typeset in 11pt on 14pt Celeste.
Origination by Amberley Publishing.
Printed in the UK.

Contents

Foreword

If you are already reading this and haven't purchased this book ... stop right now. Go to the till and buy a copy. If, however, you are already the fortunate owner, then you are in for a treat.

Even if you know nothing about the Great War Display Team right now, by the end of this account of their exploits, you will feel as if you have been in the cockpit with them and taken part in their recreation of the aerial melees that took place over the trenches.

Ernie's book is beautifully written, clear and descriptive of exactly why aircraft of the Great War were so temperamental, and why they were so difficult to handle in the deadly individual duels that ensued in the infancy of aerial combat.

This book also pays homage to members of the display team who have lost their lives engaging in their passion for flight, and who paid the ultimate price.

These aircraft are not toys. They are faithful replicas of lethal fighting machines. As the proud owner of the late John Day's magnificent Fokker DR1 Triplane, I had the privilege to fly one display season with the Team.

Their professionalism is second to none – essential given the safety constraints and associated limitations surrounding antique fighters with eccentric flying characteristics.

Every summer the team takes to the skies, and if you get a chance to see them, they perform a stunning display.

Sadly for me, my work commitments make it difficult for me to carve out the time to join them on a regular basis. Nevertheless, I am still constantly asked about what it is like to dogfight a Sopwith triplane, or how it feels to land the Fokker triplane.

I now have a 'Get Out of Jail Free' card. I can simply hand them this book and say, 'Read this, and you will understand.'

Bruce Dickinson

Introduction

I suppose this book should really be called 'My Time Flying with the Great War Display Team'. I first joined the team in 1997 and at that time there were still three founder members involved with the team. Doug Gregory and Des Biggs were regular members who continued flying with the team for many years and Ken Garrett still occasionally turned up. Chris Mann, who had flown several of the aircraft, regularly flew Ken's SE5a at displays. My old friend Robin Bowes had died two years previously but he had told me many stories about the team. Nick O'Brien, who was flying the black Fokker Dr1 at that time owned by the Museum of Army Flying, had been involved for some time and knew all the pilots. All of these people were my sources, from whom I learned the history of the team before I joined. Thankfully, many are still around and they have all delved into their memories and logbooks to provide me with information to help me research this book.

It is very easy when writing the history of anything to get bogged down in trivia; to try to make sure that every pilot and every event gets a mention. What you end up with is pages and pages of facts rather than a story, so what I have tried to write is the story of the Great War Display Team rather than the definitive history. I have tried to mention all the long-term members of the team and their aircraft, and so some of the more transient members may not have been included. I apologise for any omissions.

The team has been a large part of my life for over twenty years and continues to be so despite the fact that I retired from flying with them in 2016. I am still involved with the team, however. I now run the website and keep the server up to date so that airshow organisers can be supplied with whatever paperwork they need, so I am still involved with the day-to-day running of the team during the season. I assume it was for this reason that Amberley asked me to write this book; they thought I might know something about the subject. I hope they are right, and I hope you enjoy the story I aim to tell.

All photographs featured are the author's unless otherwise stated. My thanks to all the photographers who have let me use their pictures.

Chapter One

A Few Words about First World War Aircraft

When you consider that the First World War started in July 1914, which was only ten and a half years after the Wright brothers' first flight, it is no surprise to find that the aircraft that were flying at the beginning of the war were very basic. The laws of aerodynamics were not fully understood at that time and aircraft were still being designed on the basis of 'if it looks right it will fly right'! Unfortunately, many didn't.

Engines were also relatively new. The first internal-combustion engine that could run continuously was built in 1862, and it was only in 1885 that Gottlieb Daimler built something we might recognise today as a petrol engine. Making an engine that was light and powerful enough to get an aeroplane into the air was another challenge that had to be overcome. By the outbreak of war, few aero engines were capable of producing much more than 100 hp, with many producing just 25–30 hp. As an illustration, Louis Bleriot's monoplane, in which he staggered across the English Channel in 1909 at around 250 feet, was powered by a 25-hp engine.

At the beginning of the First World War, Britain impressed all privately owned aircraft for war service, although few would have been much more than underpowered playthings, barely capable of flight. This would explain the initial attitude of the generals who were running the war, who believed that aircraft had no part to play in warfare. They had to be persuaded that an 'eye in the sky', which could see what the enemy's troops were doing, and also where our shells were falling in relation to the enemy, might be useful. Even then, of course, there was no way of communicating between aircraft and the ground, so they either had to wait until the aircraft landed or the aircrew had to resort to throwing weighted messages over the side!

As engines became lighter, more powerful and more reliable, and the airframes became more robust and capable, more roles became available to aircraft. They could stay up for longer and fly further and higher behind enemy lines, even taking photographs of the enemy's positions using primitive but effective cameras. As both sides were doing this it soon became apparent that there was a need to keep the enemy's aircraft away from your side, so pilots on both sides started taking their revolvers, or possibly a rifle, up with them to take potshots at enemy pilots in an effort to scare them away.

Fitting a machine gun was a logical progression from this, but of course there was a problem. With most aircraft being tractor-engined (i.e. the engine in front, pulling the aircraft along), then if the gun was mounted in front of the pilot, where he could easily aim it at an enemy, it would likely blow the propeller apart. Instead, they were initially mounted on the top wings, where they could fire outside the propeller disc. This worked, but was not terribly accurate.

In 1915 the Germans started fitting interrupter gear to a machine gun fitted to a Fokker Eindecker. Although the Eindecker was not a very agile aircraft, the pilot's ability to look along his gun's barrel and aim it accurately proved to be a master stroke. Thus began what came to be known as the Fokker Scourge, with the Eindeckers shooting down huge numbers of British aircraft.

Obviously the Allies also needed an interrupter gear and various types were tried, with varying levels of success. Sopwith's Pup and Triplane were fitted with a Sopwith-Kauper system in 1916, which like the Fokker system relied on mechanical gears driven from the engine to push the safety catch off when a propeller blade was in front of the gun. Judging by the repaired hole in a Camel propeller at the Fleet Air Arm Museum at Yeovilton, it didn't always work!

It was not until 1917 when the more reliable hydraulically operated Constantinesco gear was fitted to British aircraft that things would improve. This gear allowed far higher rates of fire because the synchronisation was much more accurate, giving the Allied pilots improved chances of shooting down a German plane.

Sopwith Triplane. (John Bilcliffe)

Apart from advances in armament, everything else to do with aviation was developing at a terrific rate. There is nothing quite like a war to stimulate engineering improvements! As one side came up with a new aircraft, the other side had to have something to equal or better it. Just like with modern computers, an aircraft could go from being cutting edge to obsolete in six months as the opposition came up with something better. The Sopwith Triplane, derived from the earlier Pup, was considered in 1917 to be a vast improvement on anything available to either side and it cut a swathe through the opposition's contemporary Albatrosses, Pfalz and suchlike, but six months later it was withdrawn for home defence as being outdated.

The aircraft that were flying on both sides of the action at the time of the Armistice were virtually unrecognisable from the pathetic examples that had staggered into the air at the start of the war. Ailerons had replaced wing-warping; more powerful, reliable and lightweight engines had replaced the hugely inefficient and heavy power plants of the early days; and less draggy airframes, including monoplanes, were replacing the multi-wing types with numerous struts and bracing wires. Even the bracing wires themselves had been replaced by streamlined ones, which reduced drag.

Avro 504. (Carly Hodges)

BE2c. (John Bilcliffe)

Sopwith Triplane take
off. (Carly Hodges)

Fokker Triplanes.
(Steve Bridgewater/
Awyr Aviation
Communications)

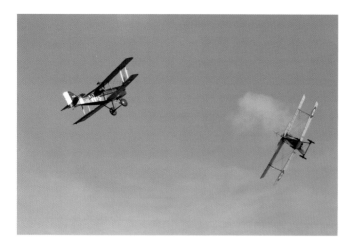

SE5as.

Junkers CL1. (Steve
Bridgewater/Awyr Aviation
Communications)

Having said all that, even the aircraft that were around in 1918 would still be considered primitive by more modern standards. Pilot comfort and safety were not high on the list of priorities of aircraft designers; one example of this is the fact that British pilots were never allowed to carry parachutes 'in case they might have been tempted to abandon an aircraft which might have been recovered and re-used'. I wonder how many pilots burned to death as a result of that decision, made of course by non-flying senior staff. Even seat belts were pretty rudimentary and unlikely to be of much use in the event of a crash. There was a story that Raymond Collishaw of No. 10 Squadron RNAS (later air vice-marshal, RAF), the Canadian ace famous for his Black Flight of Sopwith Triplanes, was once catapulted out of his cockpit and only survived because he grabbed the cabane struts of his Triplane and managed to climb back inside.

Modern pilots assume that their aeroplanes will allow them a good view of where they are going, the aerofoil sections of their wings will give them the best lift and gentlest stall available, and the controls will be light, co-ordinated and efficient.

Very restricted visibility.

None of these were guaranteed, or even likely, in a First World War aircraft. If the designer needed to mount a wing, machine gun or engine directly ahead of the pilot, then that is where it would be mounted; pilots just had to learn to cope with what they were given. Wings, whether ahead, above or below, can block out vast areas of sky. Indeed, one of the reasons given for Sopwith producing the Triplane, which has the same fuselage and identical wing area as the Pup, was to improve the view! The Pup had a wing of 5-foot chord stretching forward from just above your head, whereas the Triplane's top wing was only 3 feet 3 inches (two-thirds the length of the chord) and 3 feet higher above, giving a much improved view of anyone diving down from above. The fact that you also had another wing directly in front of your eyes was of minor significance.

The vast majority of First World War aircraft had tailskids, so the pilot's view on the ground was basically of the patch of sky above the engine. Any view ahead is whatever you can sneak by looking down either side of the engine – always assuming there isn't a wing in the way. I've often commented, when taxiing and landing modern aircraft, that they frighten the life out of me – I'm not used to being able to see where I'm going!

Stall characteristics were what they were – get used to it! The Sopwith Triplane had a reasonably gentle 1G stall with the centre of pressure seeming to move back from wing to wing until it finally gave up, but if stalled in a tight turn it would tuck under, which could be immensely thrilling at 200 feet. Both the current Fokker Dr1s have had instances where, on flying into another aircraft's wake, they simply stop flying and drop out of the sky – again, something to be avoided at low level.

As a sweeping generalisation, the most important control on a First World War aircraft is the rudder. In many cases the ailerons are relatively puny and the secondary effect of rudder gives better roll control than the primary effect of aileron. Andy Sephton, at the time chief pilot at the Shuttleworth Collection, once told me that this was because in those days they assumed that you turned using rudder, like in a boat, and the ailerons were only required to balance the rudder. In the 1915 edition of the manual *Erecting and Aligning 80 hp AVRO Biplanes, Type 504,* the ailerons are actually described as 'balancing flaps', and it was not until the 1919 manual entitled *How to Fly and Instruct on an Avro* that they were described as ailerons. This also explains the use of a slip bubble (basically a spirit level), which appears to work in the wrong way (left bubble requires right rudder) when compared to the modern slip ball if you try to fly like a modern pilot.

Another point about First World War aircraft is that they generally had very large propellers, which turned much more slowly (and much more efficiently) than modern ones. An 80-hp rotary engine could turn a 9-foot-diameter, very coarse pitch propeller, which would produce much more thrust than an equivalent modern engine/prop combination (see the Sopwith and Avro chapters).

So essentially the message I'm trying to get across is that flying a First World War aircraft is not like flying a modern one. Don't expect things to work as they would in a Cessna; you need a sense of humour to fly them! All the above is just a general outline of First World War aircraft; I have included more specific details in the chapters on each type.

The rudder, primary control.

CHAPTER TWO

Origins of the Great War Display Team

The Great War Display Team could be said to owe its existence to the late Jock Maitland, founder of the Biggin Hill Air Fair. Back in 1988 he invited the five owners of SE5as then on the British register to come along to the Biggin Hill Air Fair that year as a static display. Coincidentally he had also booked Robin Bowes to display his Fokker Dr1 Triplane at the show, so I assume he thought having a First World War line-up would look good – maybe even to celebrate the 70th anniversary of the end of the First World War.

Only two of these pilots had met previously, but as most of the SE5 pilots had built their aircraft themselves, they had been in touch, as homebuilders do, asking 'How did you get around this problem?' It was the first time any of them had met Robin.

I presume that while they were all sitting around, admiring each other's planes and talking about flying, someone had a bright idea: 'Why don't we cobble together some sort of dogfight, with the SE5as attacking the Fokker, or vice versa?' The SE5a pilots had already offered to do a flypast in formation, so this was an extension of that. Amazingly I happened upon a video of the show which somebody had posted on YouTube. This shows Robin taking off to do his usual solo display; then, when he had finished he cleared the area and the SEs took off and did their flypast. He then joined in with them and they had a little dogfight together.

Of course this was in the days before the dead hand of bureaucracy had invoked the reams of paperwork that every display pilot must fill in before he or she can display an aircraft. Nothing as relaxed as this would be allowed today; now, everybody has to have gained a Display Authorisation (DA) after convincing a CAA approved evaluator that he or she can fly the proposed display in a safe manner and they must have practised the display at least three times before they do it in public.

Anyway, back in 1988 – despite no DAs and no practice – fly it they did, and they obviously enjoyed themselves because they decided they might do it again. The original pilots were Des Biggs, who had built G-BMDB, Doug Gregory, who had built G-SEVA working alongside Des (they lived near each other and were the only ones who were friends before), Ken Garrett, who had built G-BIHF, Mark Ordish, who had built G-INNY, and Mark Smith, who owned G-BDWJ – the very first SE5a replica, which had been built in this country by Mike Beach in 1976. All these aircraft were built following the plans that had been drawn up in the 1960s in Canada and sold by a firm called Replica Plans. Robin was flying the Fokker Triplane G-BEFR, which had been built by Viv Bellamy in 1976 from plans drawn by Walt Redfern in America.

Left: Des Biggs's SE5a, G-BMDB. (Sheila Truscott)

Below: Doug Gregory's G-SEVA. (Doug Gregory)

Right: Doug in the RFC uniform. (Doug Gregory)

Below: The first UK SE5a, G-BDWJ.

The original SE5a line-up. (Doug Gregory)

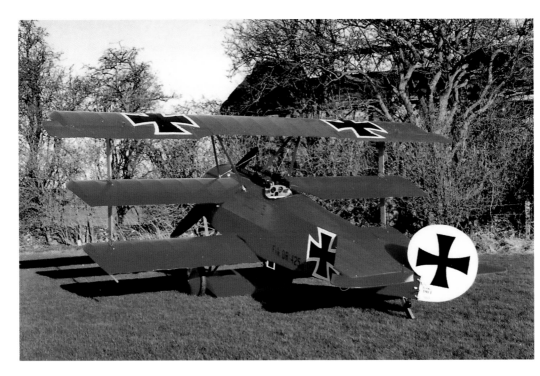

Robin Bowes' Fokker G-BEFR. (Sheila Truscott)

Robin in a German uniform. (Sheila Truscott)

It was from these disorganised beginnings that the Great War Display Team grew. It wasn't called that then, of course. In fact, the team didn't actually have a name. The second time they met up to do a display, Mark Smith, who owned a company that printed T-shirts, turned up with some with 'WOMBATS' written on them, derived from 'World War One Combat', apparently, although Des doesn't think they ever used that name officially. The name Great War Display Team first appeared much later.

The five SE5as flew together regularly, doing occasional displays either by themselves or with Robin. Mainly they flew for fun, often doing fly-pasts at local fêtes and shows for the cost of the fuel. In 1990 Chris Mann joined the group, initially as a reserve pilot. An ex-RAF pilot who flew Jumbos for BA, he had met Doug Gregory and Des Biggs at Boscombe Down and Doug let him fly G-SEVA. He went on to fly Ken Garrett's G-BIHF on a regular basis.

Judging by the entries in Chris's logbook they had a busy few years. During 1992 and 1993 they flew shows at Middle Wallop, RIAT at Fairford, Rendcombe, Popham, Headcorn, Manston (where the aircraft were fitted with miniature cameras and later featured in a TV programme narrated by Raymond Baxter), Brooklands and even as far north as Finningley (which in these small aircraft entailed two refuelling stops). This latter show, according to Chris's logbook, included three SE5as and a Sopwith Camel, which I think was owned by Tony Biancchi.

The years 1994 and 1995 were also busy, including a show at Dunkeswell in June 1994, where I was based and where I first met members of the team. During this time

Avro 504 G-ECKE. (Sheila Truscott)

The Middle Wallop Fokker G-BVGZ. (Sheila Truscott)

Robin also occasionally flew an Avro 504 G-ECKE operated by Nigel Hamlin Wright. Then sadly on 20 July 1995 Robin was killed flying his beloved Fokker at a show at Stourhead in Wiltshire. Doug, Des and Chris were circling ready to dive in after Robin opened the show with a loop, but instead he dived down, flew into a tree and crashed.

Once everyone had got over the shock of Robin's death it was decided that they should carry on. Nick O'Brien had already been flying occasionally with the team in the black Fokker Dr1, G-BVGZ, also built by Viv Bellamy and owned by the Museum of Army Flying at Middle Wallop, so he carried on being the 'filthy Hun'. Nick and Robin had even displayed together once at Rendcombe, along with Doug and Des in SE5as and Dave Starkey in the Avro.

The late 1990s saw several changes in the team. In 1997 I joined with my self-built Sopwith Triplane G-BWRA, and 1999 saw the arrival of prolific aircraft builder John Day and his building partner Bob Gauld-Galliers with their Nieuport 17 G-BWMJ. It was at about this time that the name changed. When I first joined the team,

Sopwith Triplane
G-BWRA.

John and Bob's
Nieuport, G-BWMJ.
(Sheila Truscott)

Nick O'Brien, who flew the Fokker, made all the radio calls and he used the call sign 'World War One Display Team'. Eventually he decided that was too much of a mouthful so he changed it to 'Great War Display Team' and that is what we became.

The name change coincided with another change: we gained our first manager. When I joined the team I brought with me a very useful asset – my business partner Sheila Truscott! Sheila, through her relationship with Robin Bowes, knew everyone in the airshow world and loved going to them, so she agreed to become our manager. In those days it was possibly an even more arduous task than today, because everything had to be done by telephone and mail. I recall Sheila regularly mailing off inch-thick envelopes to airshow organisers full of all the relevant documents for each pilot and aircraft.

Before Sheila took on the job I don't recall the team having any management system; I assume that the organiser of any show that wanted to book us would phone a team member he knew and ask 'Can you do a show on the...?' Even I used to get such phone calls, and I recall one which I thought was a wind-up. The caller announced that he was Group Captain Whatever from the Ministry of Defence – luckily I didn't laugh and tell him to stop ****ing about, because he *was*! He asked if I and one other British aircraft could possibly do a fly-past in France in three weeks' time. I said we would love to but it would not be possible to get the official clearance from the French that we needed to take our aircraft – which of course don't carry our official national registrations – across the Channel. He said he didn't think that would be a problem, the French Air Minister would be attending – as would Prince Charles! That was the 90th anniversary of the Battle of the Somme, which included a fly-past by myself in the Sopwith and Doug in his SE5a at the Thiepval Monument.

In 2002 the black Fokker G-BVGZ, which had previously been owned by the Army Air Corps Museum, was sold and no longer available to the team. With no German aircraft to dogfight, our display was severely limited, so as an interim John Day set about converting his Bowers Fly Baby G-BNPV (which he had built in 1987) to look like a Junkers CL1, a ground attack aircraft that arrived in the German side in 1918 – too late to take part in the war. He then set about building from scratch a Fokker Triplane of his own, G-CDXR, which first flew in 2006.

John's Fly Baby masquerading as a Junkers CL1, G-BNPV.

John's Fokker Dr1, G-CDXR, now owned by Bruce Dickinson.

Sopwith Pup
G-BZND.
(Austin Brown)

Vic Lockwood's
SE5a, G-CCBN,
now owned
by Arnd
Schweisthal.

For a few years, from 2007 to 2010, we also had a Sopwith Pup, G-BZND, which was flown by either Francis Donaldson (chief engineer of the LAA) or Dan Griffith, at the time CAA chief test pilot.

Doug and Des were by now starting to feel their ages and weren't keen on flying to shows too far away. We were lucky to have Vic Lockwood, who joined in 2007 and Dave Linney who joined in 2008 with their respective SE5as, the American-built G-CCBN and G-BDWJ, previously flown with the team by Mark Smith.

The Fokker Dr1 was not enough of a challenge for John Day, so he told me, so he decided to start building a beautiful Eindecker replica, G-CHFS, which first flew in 2012 and in which he was sadly killed the following year while practising at Middle Wallop with the team.

John's lovely Eindecker taxiing out. (Peter R. March)

An airborne shot of John's Eindecker. (Peter R. March)

After John's death his Triplane stayed with the team, having been bought by Iron Maiden lead singer Bruce Dickinson (and occasionally flown by him when his other commitments allow). The rest of the time he allows Alex Truman to fly it on his behalf.

Matthew Boddington joined in 2013. His first flight with the team in his BE2c G-AWYI was the fateful weekend when John Day was killed. Peter Bond joined the team in June 2014 flying his self-built Fokker G-CFHY, so then we had two Fokkers to shoot down.

At time of writing our latest recruits are the hugely impressive Avro 504 G-EROE, owned by Eric Roe, grandson of Alliott Verdon Roe who founded the Avro company, and we have a reappearance of G-INNY, now owned by John Gammidge but which flew at the start of the team in 1988 in the hands of its builder, Mark Ordish. We also have our first female pilot, Emily Collett, who this year has been flying Arnd's SE5a, sharing it with her husband Mike.

Matthew's BE2c,
G-AWYI. (Steve
Bridgewater/
Awyr Aviation
Communications)

Peter Bond's Fokker
Dr1, G-CFHY.

Eric Roe's Avro 504,
G-EROE.

G-INNY, one of the originals now owned by John Gammidge. (Matthew Boddington)

The current line-up at time of writing is:

Dave Linney flying his SE5a G-BDWJ
Trevor Bailey flying Mike Waldron's SE5a G-BUOD
Emily or Mike Collett flying Arnd Schweisthal's (ex-Vic Lockwood) SE5a G-CCBN
Gordon Brander flying Sopwith Triplane G-BWRA
Matthew Boddington flying BE2c G-AWYI
Alex Truman or Bruce Dickinson flying Bruce's (ex-John Day) Fokker Dr1 G-CDXR
Peter Bond flying his Fokker Dr1 G-CFHY
Will Greenwood flying Andrew Berry's (ex-John Day) Junkers CL1 G-BNPV
Mark Johnson flying Eric Verdon-Roe's Avro 504 G-EROE

Founding members of the team, Des Biggs and Doug Gregory, continued flying with them until 2012, by which time Doug was eighty-nine. He flew his beloved SE5a in 2013 on his ninetieth birthday and then sold it. Des sold his soon after and so ended the last direct links with the original team, although Mark Smith's SE5a still flies in the capable hands of Dave Linney.

CHAPTER THREE

The Sopwith Aircraft

After leasing my garage business to a friend in 1988, I started working on aircraft, which I enjoyed much more than working on cars. I did much of the work in Robin Bowes' hangar-like workshop at Ermington, alongside Robin and Dave Silsbury.

One lunchtime in 1993 we were sitting around discussing what to build next and Robin suggested something from the First World War which could be displayed alongside his Fokker Dr1. Dave had heard about the wreckage of a Sopwith Triplane replica which had been built as a two-seater by John Penney several years before and had been written off in a landing accident. That was the start! Without the help of both Robin and Dave, the Triplane would probably not exist.

Three years after starting, I had built a new fuselage and fitted a 165-hp Warner Scarab radial engine, which was much more like the original rotary than the Lycoming that had previously powered it. I had also completely rebuilt the wings and re-rigged them, which was no mean feat. There are four variables on each wing – gap, stagger, dihedral and incidence – and getting all four correct on six wings took me six weeks. I now had a complete Sopwith Triplane replica.

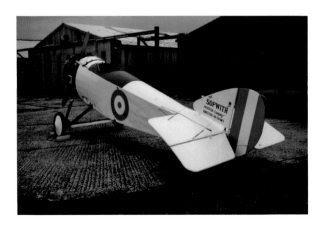

The completed Sopwith fuselage.

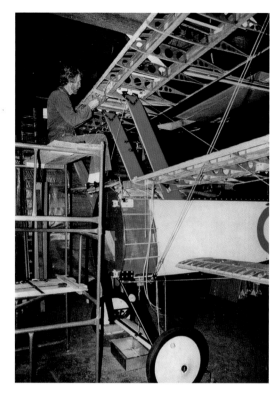

Left: Rigging the Sopwith wings.

Below: Sopwith at Yeovilton.

The original reason for building the Triplane was to fly at airshows alongside Robin, who also owned a half-share in the aircraft. Sadly Robin was killed flying his Fokker in 1995 and I had to move the Sopwith out of his workshop. By then the fuselage was complete, the engine installed and running and the wings built and rigged, but not covered and painted.

After his death, Robin's share in the aircraft was bought out by his girlfriend, Sheila Truscott. She became my business partner and later became our manager, contacting airshow organisers and arranging displays for us. She had spent most of her time with Robin travelling to shows and knew all the pilots and organisers, so this was a way of continuing to do something she enjoyed immensely.

In order to make the plane look a little different from most First World War aircraft, I had opted to paint it to represent N500, the first Sopwith prototype, which flew to France in clear-doped linen in June 1916 rather than the green or brown drab in which most were painted.

The first test flight took place in August of 1996 in the hands of Dave Starkey, who had done the stress analysis on the airframe and who was also a very experienced pilot of First World War aircraft. Apart from complaining that the seat was unbelievably uncomfortable and needed adjustment, Dave was happy with the way the aircraft flew and filled in the test report for the then Popular

Clear-doped linen.

Sopwith arriving at Culdrose. (Sheila Truscott)

Flying Association, now called the Light Aircraft Association. They are the people in charge of overseeing the home-building of aircraft. Once they were satisfied that the aircraft was safe to fly and had no nasty surprises for an inexperienced pilot, I was allowed my first flight on 6 September 1996.

Although I had sat in the cockpit countless times (pretending to fly, as you do!), it was not until I taxied and took off that I realised just how awful the view from the cockpit was. As for landing, the realisation that I could see nothing forward or downward on final approach was something of a shock. Despite this, both myself and the aircraft survived my first flight, and I loved the challenge of flying it.

Now, what was I going to do with the aircraft? It was uncomfortable, expensive to run, the lack of visibility meant it was not the sort of thing to take to a fly-in at a farm strip and, as it had a tail skid and no brakes, it could only land on grass. I already had a Display Authorisation, which I had never actually used, but despite my total lack of experience in display flying, that was the only possible use for the aircraft. If I couldn't fly it at displays, I would have to find someone who could. I duly contacted some of the members of the team Robin had flown with to ask their advice.

They invited me to fly up to join their practice at Middle Wallop to see what I and the aircraft could do. I had briefly met Doug and Des through Robin, but the first person who greeted me was Nick O'Brien, then a major in the Army Air Corps and the pilot of the black Fokker Dr1. Doug Gregory, Des Biggs and Chris Mann turned up soon after. We discussed what we might do and then went off and flew a couple of dogfights – enormous fun for me! It seemed that I was accepted; I was now part of the team.

Wheeling it on.

Over two hectic days we flew many practice sessions and then off we went to Biggin Hill for my first ever public display. Over that weekend I flew two displays with the team at Biggin Hill and also a solo slot at Dunsfold. It was quite the baptism of fire, but I loved it.

So how did it fly? Well, nothing like a modern aeroplane; the ailerons were heavy and did little, but the rudder, although not very big, was very effective. The secondary effect of rudder produced more roll than the primary effect of the ailerons, so that became my primary control. The elevator was also powerful – made more so by the centre of gravity being near the rear limit, which always makes an aircraft twitchy in pitch. The aircraft is heavy, so hauling it around in tight turns, much needed in dogfights, was very hard work.

Of course, the biggest problem was landing; the lack of forward and downward view in the three-point attitude meaning that it was better to wheel it on so that I could see where I was going, then use the rudder with a burst of power if required to keep it straight until the speed decayed and the tail came down. After that I just had to hope there was nothing in front, because I certainly couldn't see it. However, once the skid was on the ground, it would stop fairly quickly.

If I had to three-point it, the technique was to aim it at where I had last seen the runway and hope nobody had moved it! Unfortunately on one occasion they had – I must have drifted slightly to the right on final approach and instead of landing on the closely mown runway I was landing on the 2-foot-high grass by the side. As soon as the wheels touched the tops of the grass the friction stopped them dead and the aircraft pivoted neatly around them, ending up upside down. The only good thing about landing accidents in First World War aircraft is that they usually happen fairly slowly, so while they are very embarrassing, they are also survivable.

During my research while building the Sopwith I had seen many pictures of Triplanes parked on their noses or upside down, including three separate ones of

An occupational hazard! (Mary Goddard)

N500, so crashing was obviously an occupational hazard. I ended up with it upside down once and on its nose twice.

Using the wheel-landing technique, I found the aircraft could cope with surprising amounts of crosswind; I once landed at Biggin Hill with 7–8 knots straight across the runway. The problem is of course that there is no future in constantly adding power to keep it on the runway; eventually you have to stop. But at least I could keep it under control until the speed decayed enough to allow it to swing in an area of my choosing, where there was enough room for it to happen safely.

Once on the ground the lack of brakes sometimes meant that if I wasn't sure there was still enough room left to stop I had to kick in full rudder and add a blast of power to start a ground loop – a 180-degree turn. This was risky and put enormous strain on the undercarriage, but if the alternative was hitting the hedge then I had little choice. The undercarriage, luckily, was very strong, having been over-engineered by me!

Taxiing was also tricky. It was very important when climbing in the aircraft to get a mental picture of what was ahead so that I would know, for instance, to set off with an initial swing to the right to avoid a potential hazard on the left. Once I was moving it became easier; the rudder is surprisingly powerful when allied with a blast of power and I could swing easily from side to side, allowing me a glimpse under the mid wing and down each side of the nose to see where I was going. Despite the lack of brakes I found that I could turn surprisingly quickly on the ground. Full forward stick allied with full rudder and a blast of power took the weight off the skid and the tail would swing around remarkably easily.

Gordon looking between the top and mid wings. (Steve Bridgewater/ Awyr Aviation Communications)

In the air the view forward is not wonderful but acceptable; with so many wings and struts there is always something in the way, and even in level flight it was always necessary to weave, lowering the wings one way and then the other, in order to be able to keep my eyes open for potential hazards.

Of course in the display the potential hazards are all around, with anything up to nine other aircraft in the air, but the display is carefully choreographed, so provided everyone is where they should be it is perfectly safe. Flying in formation was tricky; I needed to keep the target aircraft in a rectangle formed by the top and mid wing and the two sets of struts. If it moved up or down I had to break away because I had no idea where it was any more.

I have said before that the controls are not particularly effective and the aircraft is heavy. Having taken part in many a dogfight with the Fokker Dr1, I can only say I'm pleased they never met for real. The Fokker came into service some eighteen months later in the war, and given the speed of improvements during wartime, that represented a quantum leap in design. The Fokker is smaller and lighter, with less wing area (hence less roll inertia). It is more compact and, in aerodynamic terms, neutrally stable in roll and yaw. Stability is not a good thing in a fighting aircraft. I recall the first time I did a dogfight routine with John Day in his Fokker. We reached the end of the display line and John simply vanished! I put in all the control I had and heaved on the stick but there was absolutely no way I could catch him in the turn. In real life he could have pulled around behind and shot me down with ease.

While I am discussing dogfighting, it always amuses me when I see modern films depicting aircraft (usually computer generated these days) where they show the good guy chasing immediately behind the tail of the bad guy before giving him a blast of machine gun fire and then down he goes. Believe me, the last place you want to be is in the prop-wash immediately behind another aircraft! At best the

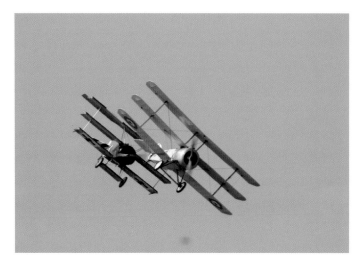

Out-manoeuvred again!

wake would knock you all over the sky, making aiming impossible; at worst the rotating air could roll you upside down and possibly put you in a spin. I recall once accidentally flying into Nick's wake at a show and very nearly doing a barrel roll at 200 feet! Not recommended. The best way to shoot someone down would be from slightly above or slightly off to one side, away from the wake.

Another point is that these early aircraft were very slow and had no reserve power to overtake another aircraft. The only way to catch someone is to dive on them, and the ideal way to bounce them is to dive out of the sun from behind them, then drop down as close to their tail as possible, haul the nose up and rake the underside of the aircraft with machine gun fire from very close range. You would be bound to hit something vital, possibly the engine, fuel or oil tank or the pilot. Whatever you hit, you would put that aircraft out of action.

To round off this section on Sopwith aircraft, in 2003 I was asked to re-engine and test-fly a Sopwith Pup. It had been built to a beautiful standard by my friend Brendan Goddard in his back garden. Sadly Brendan died, but not before he had had the chance to see his creation taxi at an airfield. He had built the replica to an authentic design and had opted to use a Salmson 80-hp radial engine because the original Pup had an 80-hp le Rhone rotary. Unfortunately for various technical reasons the Salmson could not produce anything like enough thrust to make the aircraft fly; in fact, it was barely able to taxi.

After Brendan's death, his widow, Mary, contacted me and said that Brendan had intended to ask me if I would re-engine the aircraft and get it flying for him. Would I be prepared to do so now so it could fly in his memory? Of course I said yes, and the aircraft was delivered to me in pieces. Brendan had painted the Pup to represent N5199, an aircraft that flew with Naval No. 3 Squadron at Vert Galand in early 1917.

Fitting a bigger engine was of course not quite that simple. I had a stress analysis done on the airframe and I needed to substantially beef up the front end. Then,

The Pup's engine fitted.

The first flight in the Pup.
(Derek Boyce)

having located a 145-hp Warner Scarab, I had to make a suitable engine mount, build an exhaust system, fit the engine and plumb in all the necessary systems. That took a while, as you can imagine, so its first flight took place on 12 December 2005.

So many First World War pilots extolled the virtues of the Pup, but I had been warned beforehand that there was a design flaw and they flew 'tail heavy'. On my first flight I had briefed my friends on the ground to wing-walk me to the very start of Runway 31, the longest runway at Bodmin. I had intended to apply half power, check to make sure there were no unpleasant surprises in the way the aircraft behaved before take-off, and to only then apply full power and get airborne. Good theory! After applying half power and feeling the controls, I looked over the side and realised I was already 6 feet in the air. In the circumstances I thought I may as well go flying, so I put on full power. The aircraft attempted to loop from the runway. In order to keep it to a steady climb and then level off I had to brace my shoulder against the back of the seat and push the stick forward, and that was how I did the first circuit and landing in the Pup.

Obviously the airframe needed some modification, so after consulting with Francis Donaldson, chief engineer at the LAA, who later displayed the aircraft, I raised the leading edge of the tailplane by an inch. Subsequent flights were much better, but the aircraft was very much over-engined. With the 80-hp Salmson it could barely taxi, but with the 145-hp Scarab it leapt off the ground and climbed like a Harrier – so much so that I rarely needed more than half throttle once airborne.

I did everything necessary for the official flight test regime and eventually got a full permit to fly, so the aircraft then became part of the team for a few years, until sadly Mary also died and the aircraft changed hands. In many ways it was easier to fly than the Triplane, not least because it was possible to get some forward and downward view. It also had a stall speed some 10 knots slower than the Triplane, so landing at Watchford Farm was never a problem. The ailerons, however, were terrible; obviously there were only four of them against the six on the Triplane, and they were very much smaller. This meant that they were very light and almost useless – so much so that on the first flight I tried to bank with them and actually thought for a moment 'Did I connect them?' The one thing they were very good at was demonstrating adverse yaw, something that modern instructors tell you about but find very difficult to demonstrate in modern aircraft. On the Pup, if you held the rudder central and put in full right aileron, it would roll right, yaw left and fly straight on.

One aspect of the Pup's handling that for some reason didn't apply so much to the Triplane was the fact that in a steep-banked turn it would fall into the turn, so in order to perform a steep-banked turn to the right you had to give full right rudder and balance that with right ailerons. Then, when you had achieved the necessary bank, you had to put in full opposite rudder to stop it falling in. This meant that you always flew steep-banked turns with crossed controls – in this case full right aileron and full left rudder – and yet the slip bubble was centred, meaning that the aircraft was in balance. I never worked out quite how that could be.

I sold the Triplane in 2010 to Gordon Brander, a team member who had previously been flying John Day's Junkers CL1, and I supposedly retired from display flying. After fourteen years with the team, accruing some 360 hours on Sopwith aircraft, I had come to realise that I lived in the wrong part of the country. Most airshows are in the South East and for me living in Plymouth that meant long transit times, often in deteriorating weather, to get back to Watchford Farm, followed by an hour and more driving home. In all, the total travelling time was exhausting at my advancing age. I missed the thrill of flying with the team and I missed meeting old friends at the shows, but I didn't miss the hours of travel.

I thought that was the end of my displaying career, but it was not to be – see the section on the SE5a.

CHAPTER FOUR

Fokker Dr1

When the Sopwith Triplane first appeared on the Western Front in mid-1916, it proved far superior in climb and manoeuvrability to the German aircraft of the time, particularly the Albatros DIII. Idflieg ordered a Triplane design in an effort to counter the Sopwith. Many German manufacturers put forward designs but the winner was the Dutch company headed by Anthony Fokker. While researching this book I read a write-up featured in Jane's *Fighting Aircraft of the First World War* about a captured Fokker Dr1 written by M. Lagorgette for *L'Aerophile* magazine in 1917, which states that it is 'in effect a copy of the Sopwith Triplane', and saying that it had been introduced because the Albatrosses were 'unable to spin round or loop in the same small radius which is possible in the lighter British fighting machines'. The Fokker is certainly able to do that!

It is totally wrong to describe it as a copy of the Sopwith as their construction is completely different. The Fokker has three self-supporting cantilever wings of narrowing span with no dihedral, which are bolted to the cabane struts, the fuselage top and the fuselage bottom in turn. It has interplane struts, but they are really just jury struts put in to counter vibrations rather than load-bearing struts like a biplane. There are, of course, no bracing wires.

The Sopwith in comparison has six separate wings mounted and rigged using cabane and interplane struts, with flying and landing wires, which take the loads. The Sopwith is in fact rigged as a biplane, with the flying and landing wires cutting through the structure of the mid wing. The wing section is much thinner, and hence less draggy, than the Fokker. All six wings have ailerons, whereas the Fokker only has them on the top wing.

Because the Fokker has no dihedral and no fixed fin, it is neutrally stable in roll and yaw. By then designers had realised that stability is not good in a fighting aircraft. This helps the Fokker to be much more manoeuvrable than the Sopwith – having tried to dogfight one I can only say that I'm happy they never met for real; the Sopwith would not stand a chance against the far more nimble, more heavily armed Fokker.

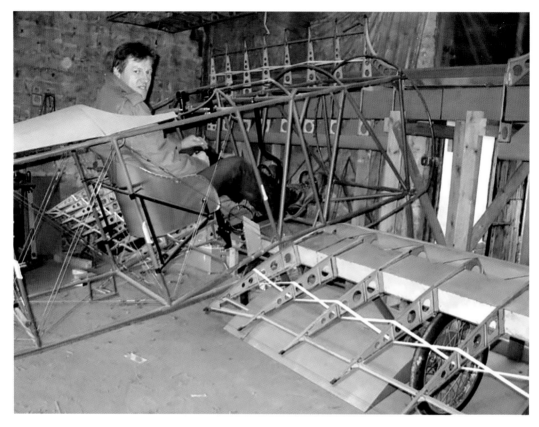

Peter Bond pretending to fly with only one wing fitted. (Peter Bond)

For such an unusual aeroplane, I was amazed to realise that they have been the second most plentiful type in the team, beaten only by the SE5a. Robin Bowes' G-BEFR (painted to represent one of the planes flown by Manfred von Richtofen) was the first, right from the start of the team, followed by the black ex-Museum of Army Flying G-BVGZ, which joined at the time Robin was killed in July 1995. Next came John Day's version, G-CDXR (painted to represent a Fokker flown by Leutnant Johannes Janzen in 1918), and finally Peter Bond's G-CFHY (replicating that flown by Leutnant Ludwig Beckmann of Jasta 6).

Robin and his Fokker were my introduction to First World War aircraft and, ultimately, the Great War Display Team. I had known Robin for many years because we both worked in the motor trade in Plymouth and had several mutual friends. In 1983 Robin had taken me flying in a Rallye he then owned and that was me hooked – I simply had to learn to fly. Having learned to fly I kept bumping into him, often with his Fokker, at various local airfields. I was entranced by his stories about flying this machine in various displays. I always remember him telling me about his first ever flight in it after he and his partner Pat Crawford had bought it. He did a circuit in it, landed, and said 'It's bloody horrible, Crawford, let's sell it!'

Robin's Triplane.
(Sheila Truscott)

The Middle Wallop
Dr1. (Sheila Truscott)

Bruce's Triplane.

Peter's Triplane.

Robin in the wreckage
after the crash in
Germany. (Sheila
Truscott)

Despite that he persevered and grew to love his quirky machine. I started
working on aircraft at his workshop around the time he had had an engine failure
in Germany on his way to an air show. At the time he was flying over miles and
miles of forest and when the engine stopped he saw a tiny patch of grass, which
was not really big enough but it had to do. He got the plane down but ran out of
space. The German fire brigade had to saw the wings off in order to recover it.
I saw some German TV footage where he was interviewed alongside his wrecked
Fokker and he was almost in tears.

I was involved in the complete rebuild, helping him repair the steel-tube fuselage
and fit the new engine mount while another friend, Dave Silsbury, built three new
box-spars for the wings. The Fokker is an immensely strong design, but relatively
light. Robin's was built using Walt Redfern's plans, whereas both the current ones

An interplane strut. (Peter Bond)

in the team are from Ron Sand's plans – I have no idea what difference there is, although from what I have read the Sand plans are easier to build. The three wings are cantilevered, each bolted on to the fuselage and capable of taking whatever loads are thrown at them.

Unlike the Sopwith, the 'interplane struts' are virtually there for show. Reinhold Platz, who was involved in the design of the Dr1, said in an interview in 1959 that they carry very little load, only being fitted to stop wing vibrations. He also mentioned, but failed to confirm, the rumour that they were fitted because it was felt that pilots used to biplanes with interplane struts felt uneasy seeing the wings with nothing between them and Fokker, being a good salesman, fitted the struts to please them.

Having talked to Robin and Nick O'Brien, and more recently both Alex and Peter in the team, this lack of positive stability means the pilot has to fly the aircraft at all times – it cannot be flown hands-off. As with the Sopwith, the rudder is the most important control both for yaw and roll. The ailerons are heavy and not particularly useful, although they are very good at demonstrating adverse yaw.

Both Alex and Peter have experienced a strange phenomenon in the Fokkers: if they fly into wake turbulence, they can simply stop flying. Peter said that first you notice that the ailerons stop working completely, followed by a nose drop. At the low levels the team operate at this is a problem, but as soon as the plane is clear of

The very restricted view from Peter's Fokker.

the wake turbulence it is a simple matter of unloading the wings and then pulling back up to level flight again, albeit with a much higher pulse rate.

Another point that Peter makes, which applies to most of these aircraft, is that nil wind is almost the worst possible situation for landing. If there is a wind, even a strong one, this causes no problem as long as you land as close to the wind direction as possible. With no wind to give directional stability and the rudder blanked by the fuselage in the three-point attitude, there is nothing to keep the aircraft on track, and the slightest bump or tussock of grass can be enough to cause it to wander off in a different direction. For this reason I always used to keep a trickle of power on to provide a bit of draught over the rudder and fin until I was certain I had the plane under control and it was slow enough to need no power in order to stop.

The following comes from a flight report Peter wrote after his first flight in his Fokker:

The aeroplane was built, using Ron Sands drawings, over a five-year period starting in April 2005, in one of the outbuildings adjoining my house; namely a 200 year old barn, which was just big enough to house the fully assembled Triplane.

Peter avoiding the flak. (Neil Woodhouse)

While taxiing the view is very much restricted by the centre wing, with only a very small segment visible through the cutout areas. Turning needed full rudder with bursts of power while unloading the tailskid with forward stick. My aircraft is fitted with disc brakes but even using these is not enough to perform a tight 180 to face the take-off direction.

I pushed the throttle smoothly forward, initially with the stick held back, but easing it forward to neutral once we were moving. The tail came up quite quickly and now I could see ahead. As I was registering this fact the aeroplane became airborne. I was flying!

I had not had to do much with the rudder during the take-off, and I was now climbing away. A quick glance at the slip ball showed it in the middle. Airspeed was about 60 mph.

Peter landing at Duxford after the show. (John Bilcliffe)

At about 1,000 feet I started a turn to the left. As soon as I applied aileron, I realized this aeroplane was different. I suddenly had a fierce draught on the left of my face, and was reminded that I had not pulled my goggles down from my forehead before take-off. I pulled my goggles down and looked at the slip ball. It was full scale left. I eased in some left rudder to balance and the nose seemed to tuck under in a sort of incipient spiral dive. I was facing roughly the way I wanted to go so I raised the nose and levelled the wings, eyes back to the slip ball. Slightest touch on the rudder and the ball was back in the centre. The rudder is god on this machine.

I had 2,100 RPM set and was doing 80 mph indicated but I must have been climbing because when I looked at the altimeter again I was at 1,500 feet. Time for another turn to the left. A bit of aileron and a little left rudder, there's that side draught again – slip ball full scale left – more rudder – down goes the nose – ease off the aileron – pick the nose up – leave the rudder on....slip ball in the middle. Phew! This is not like a Pitts. Ok, let's try one to the right. This time I led with rudder and followed with aileron, which was much better. I managed to keep it more or less in balance.

From what I had done so far, the ailerons seemed quite heavy, the elevator about right and the rudder very light. Since the rudder was all flying without a fin, I suspect it would flick to full left or right if one's feet were taken off the rudder bar, resulting in some very interesting attitudes very quickly. I'll let you know... (It doesn't!)

It was now time to try out some slow speed handling in preparation for the landing. I was still up at 2,000 feet and after a quick look around throttled back and let the speed bleed off to the point of stall. A little buffet and the nose gently dropped

Fokkers ganging up on the poor Sopwith!

at about 45 mph indicated. I increased the power to recover with very little height loss and then tried another to make sure. No tendency to drop a wing with power off stalls.

Right, time to make a practice approach. Height down to 600 feet. I positioned myself for a final approach to the same bit of grass I had taken off from. Watch the slip ball in that final turn, speed was now stabilized at 60 mph, which felt right with a good view of the field between the two Spandaus. A good hard look at the windsock. Right on the nose. I came down to about 50 feet and slowly opened up to go around. I flew level for the cameras and then climbed back to 600 feet, happy with the practice approach, and decided that if all looked good on the next one, I would land off it. The next approach was a carbon copy of the first with the speed easily stabilized at 60 with a little power left on. Windsock still looking good. I brought the Triplane down and when I thought the height was right began to ease the stick back and reduced the power to idle in unison. As the machine began to sink I kept the stick coming back and we touched down softly in a three point attitude with just a small skip and very short roll out. I had not had to do anything with the rudder after touchdown, the rollout was that short.

Alex Truman, who has flown both Sopwith and Fokker many times, makes these observations:

The performance of the Sopwith and Fokker are very similar in climb and cruise, with the Sopwith just having the edge in climb. In terms of handling they are both directionally unstable. That said with no fixed fin area the Fokker is much worse and keeping the ball somewhere near the middle is a constant task, even in straight and level transits one is constantly making tiny subconscious corrections.

Nothing can be seen forward in either of them on the ground however in the Fokker once the tail is up the view is pretty good, with your sight line above the mid wing. The Sopwith mid wing is about level with your eyes, with the tail up in the Sopwith you still can't see forwards and regular small bunts are necessary on transits to navigate and see the sky/ground in front of you. In the Sopwith one sits lower in the Cockpit, with the windscreen larger and closer. Consequently one is slightly more out of the elements and it can be flown comfortably without goggles. By contrast in the Fokker unless I bend forward into the lee of the machine guns/cockpit coaming I am constantly battered by the airflow, goggles are an absolute necessity and having them blow off would leave you in real difficulties.

As mentioned above, both the Sopwith and Fokker are very similar in climb and cruise, with the Sopwith just having the edge in climb, although Pete's Dr1 will eat them both for breakfast (Peter's Fokker, like Robin's after the rebuild, has a 180-hp Lycoming engine, which is much lighter and more powerful than the Warner Scarab Radial on both the Sopwith and Bruce's Fokker, so it would easily outperform both). They both have plenty of performance, however, and are by no means underpowered.

The Fokker clearly manoeuvres much more quickly, despite having a third of the number of ailerons. It feels much more robust in the air and on the ground, probably because it is actually three cantilever wings with box spars not relying on a maze of wires for drag, anti-drag, flying and landing loads. A much stiffer structure all round. The undercarriage is immensely strong but rather stiff; if the aeroplane starts to bounce on landing, a bit of drift allied to a rather high centre of gravity can cause things to get alarming very quickly. By contrast the Sopwith undercarriage soaks up rough ground very well and will flatter all but the most awful arrival.

CHAPTER FIVE

Avro 504

The Avro 504 was actually an amazing machine. First designed and test flown in 1913, it continued in production and operational service until 1932, with over 10,000 being built, including those licence-built in Japan and Russia.

It was originally designed as a front-line fighting aircraft, capable of carrying guns and bombs. One of its early successes was one of the first strategic bombing raids in history, when three RNAS Avro 504s flew to Friedrichshafen and bombed the Zeppelin sheds in November 1914, damaging the sheds and destroying the hydrogen production plant. In the front-line role it was soon obsolete, although some were armed with a single Lewis gun on the top wing, being used as Home Defence aircraft in 1917.

It really scored as a training aircraft and it was in this role as standard trainer for the RAF (and many other air forces), fitted with a wide variety of engines from the Gnome 80-hp rotary it had been designed for up to the 160-hp Armstrong-Siddely Lynx radial, that it continued until 1932.

The team Avro was built in Argentina by Pur Sang Aero Historic in 2010 and is owned by Eric Verdon Roe – grandson of Sir Alliott Verdon Roe, who started the Avro Aircraft Company, which had originally built the 504. Pur Sang's interest in the 504 was that the newly formed Air Force of Argentina was equipped with ten Avro 504K Gosports, bought from A. V. Roe & Co. in kit form in 1925 and assembled in Argentina. So there was a particular affection for the marque and Pur Sang have also constructed several static 504 replicas for museums. This aircraft is powered by a Rotec nine-cylinder R3600 150-hp radial engine in place of the original rotary engine.

The first impression a watcher gets of the Avro is that it is majestically slow; indeed, it gives the impression of wafting gently into the air. It is far larger than any other team aircraft and much slower; even the SE5as have to resort to performing S-turns to stay behind it.

The team's Avro with its Rotec radial.

The physical size of the aeroplane.

Wafting gently into the air. (Carly Hodges)

Far larger than any other team aircraft. (Carly Hodges)

The Junkers and SE5a performing S-turns to stay behind it.

The following was taken from an article written by Matthew Boddington for *Aeroplane Monthly*:

A book could be written about how difficult it was to import the 504K, but S/N 002 registration LV-X 430 was finally released from customs just in time to appear at the Goodwood Revival in September 2013. It was early June 2015 when Eric made the decision to move the aircraft to Sywell under the care of Matthew Boddington, part-owner and pilot of the BE2c 'Biggles Biplane' who had been responsible for the rebuild. The aeroplane had an electric system, which of course the original did not and, for ease of operation, had disc brakes fitted.

The work required by the UK authorities had now been completed but unfortunately there was still a small snag, the aircraft was still not registered in the UK and this could not happen until it had been removed from the Argentinian register. There was another long period of waiting for the Argentinian authorities to confirm that the 504 had been de-registered and provided the correct paperwork. This finally arrived in early February 2016 and she was placed on the UK register as G-EROE.

Eric had decided that he wanted the aeroplane to represent a civilian 504 rather than wear a military scheme. This would mean that the aeroplane would have large registration across the top wings, however down the fuselage Eric wanted the wording AVRO as many 504's had during the 20's. This required an application to be made to the CAA for a dispensation to not display a fuselage registration. Now although it is standard for the CAA to issue dispensation to carry military markings it is not to issue dispensation for an unusual civilian scheme!! The CAA registration people were very understanding but they were in unknown territory, at this moment in time they have given us a temporary dispensation to carry the AVRO logo pending further evidence of 504s in the 20s carrying the logo so if anyone out there has any photos we would love you to get in touch.

Finally in April 2016, almost three years after the aircraft had arrived in the UK it was cleared to fly with the issue of its first Permit Flight Release Certificate. All that was needed now was for the weather gods to play ball, again we waited for the right day and finally on the evening of the 5th of May 2016 she finally took to the UK skies from Sywell for the first time.

Above: Dan Griffith, dwarfed by the size of the machine.

Right: The Avro, making the Junkers look tiny.

The Rotec radial under a big, round cowling.

The undercarriage, with its wooden skid.

The first thing that strikes people as they walk up to the 504 is the physical size of the aeroplane, at 36 foot span, 29 foot in length and over 10 foot high it's a big aeroplane, certainly if you compare it to its Second World War equivalent the Tiger Moth.

The front of the aircraft is dominated by the big round cowling hiding the Rotec radial engine and the large wooden Skid that sticks out the front of the aeroplane, a common feature of Aircraft just before and during the early years of the First World War.

Pre-flighting the aircraft ready for flight is mainly taken up with the preparation of the Rotec radial engine. As with any Radial engine the main concern is oil build up in the lower cylinders, three manifold drains are fitted to the cylinder intake tubes and these need to be opened to drain any accumulation of engine oil. With the drains open the propeller is pulled through at least one turn for each cylinder to make sure that no oil remains in the lower cylinders.

The walk around of the airframe is all very standard stuff but you are immediately made aware of the myriad of struts and wires that hold the thing together, all of which need to be checked for their correct tension and that they are securely in place. Clambering up into the rear cockpit again gives you the impression of the size of the aeroplane and for those with shorter legs it's quite a reach to get your foot into the step on the lower fuselage side! Once installed in the seat and firmly strapped in, the fuel and oil cocks on the port and stbd sides of the fuselage are moved to the on position. The starting procedure for the Rotec is somewhat different from the original rotary engine and is a self-contained affair rather than requiring the assistance of a prop swinger!

With the fuel pump energised to prime the engine and the choke moved to the fully closed position the engine starter can be pushed, at least 5 full revolutions of the prop to check for hydraulicing and then the ignition switches can be moved to the on position. If all is well the Rotec will burst into life and settle into a gentle purr once the choke is moved to open.

Once the engine has been allowed to warm up the usual mag checks etc. can be carried out before the chocks are waved away. Although chocks are normally used the wheel brakes are more than adequate to hold the aircraft at engine run up.

Taxiing the aeroplane to take off requires care in anything but complete calm conditions as even with the wheel brakes the fully castoring tailskid will cause the aeroplane to try and weather cock at every opportunity. That said the rudder is very effective and with care and anticipation the 504 can be kept under some form of control!

The take-off is carried out into the prevailing wind, opening the throttle causes a reasonably rapid acceleration followed by what can only be described as a levitating into the air. The climb out is somewhat sedate as the modern power plant is somewhat of a retrograde step, the increased reliability is at a price in that the new power plant is unable to swing a propeller of the original size and the performance certainly suffers. That said once airborne the replica 504 is a delight and immediately brings a smile to the face. That is as long as you don't want to get anywhere too quickly, a sedate 55/60 mph cruise is what you get and the controls are as you would expect from this era, ailerons that are best described as interesting and best used to balance

Just about to touch down.

rather than initiate the turn, elevators that are light and a VERY powerful rudder. Turns are best done in a reasonable flat attitude as too high a bank angle will cause the aeroplane to slide uncontrollably into the turn; not good if you are low down.

The landing approach is a very slow affair and care is needed to allow for the drag of all those struts and wires, height is kept until close in and can soon be lost; in the event of an engine failure you won't be gliding very far that's for sure! A slow touchdown and a roll of a few yards, as the tail touches down and the stick is pulled into your stomach you feel the blade at the rear of the long skid under the aeroplane dig into the grass and arrest your progress.

As you taxi back to the hangar and then sit there going through the shutdown process you cannot help but have a grin on your face and the theme tune to 'Wings' whistling in your ears.

Since gaining its permit, the 504 has acquired over seventy hours of flying and she joined the Great War Display Team in 2017. Some comments from Mark Johnson, who currently flies the Avro in the team:

Cockpit access to the rear is good, with two steps built into the fuselage, however some dexterity is needed to get into the front as it is underneath the centre-section, between the centre-section struts. Once installed, the cockpit itself is very roomy. There is no floor so what is dropped is lost. Both seats are non-adjustable, with a high metal back and a leather seat cushion and are one of the most comfortable aircraft seats I have ever used. The Avro screen provides adequate protection from the slipstream but I always use goggles.

The two steps required to get into the rear cockpit.

On the ground the 504 needs care, especially in any sort of wind. The view from the cockpit is good, however the track is narrow, the centre of gravity high and there is a lot of lightly loaded wing area. The rudder is effective with a little slipstream, this aircraft is fitted with brakes and, in windy conditions, the ailerons can be used as airbrakes to assist with turning. It is better to have wing-walkers on hand to assist with any close manoeuvring. Take-off is straightforward. The elevators are light and effective and the tail can be raised immediately. The rudder, too, is light and can easily counter any swing. The actual lift-off is always a delight as the low speed gives the sensation of a gentle levitation from the ground. I would recommend always operating into the wind, however, a slight crosswind can be countered with into-wind aileron.

Climb is sedate, various manuals say between 50 and 55 mph, however I use the high side in case of engine failure. With full power and the present engine/prop combination climb rate, one up, and full fuel, is around 380 fpm. A note on speeds. Stall is 33 mph, with a little aerodynamic buffet before the event; cruising speed is 57 mph; approach speed is 55 mph (books vary between 50 and 60 mph); and maximum speed is 85 mph.

Once at a safe altitude, the controls are as one would expect, the elevators are light and pleasant, the rudder is light to operate but across the speed-range there is a slight

A much better forward view than for many in the team.

lag between application of the control and the reaction of the aeroplane. What would come more as a surprise to modern flyers are the ailerons, or 'balancing flaps' as they are called in the manual 'Erecting and Aligning 80hp AVRO Biplanes, Type 504'.

There are four ailerons, operated via cables and pulleys in a closed-loop system. There is no differential so the aircraft displays aileron drag although this can be easily controlled with rudder. The ailerons are heavy and the roll reaction slow. Turns are made in the usual co-ordinated way, 'bank, balance, back-pressure' however I am always very conservative in any turns close to the ground. The best method is to perform a co-ordinated turn but turning with the rudder and balancing with the ailerons thus producing a slight skidding turn and eliminating the possibility of sideslip close to the deck. There is no elevator trim and, like most early aircraft, the 504 is a little tail heavy throughout the c of g range.For the approach and landing an approach speed of 55mph is comfortable, providing enough airflow over the ailerons for adequate lateral control. The optimum technique is to stay close into the field on the downwind and fly a curved approach from abeam the threshold, maintaining a little power right through the round-out. The high drag will cause the 504 to run up the back of the drag curve very quickly so as soon as the power is reduced the aircraft will settle onto the ground.

Some judgement is needed to achieve a smooth landing, the bungee cord shock absorbers will bounce the aircraft if you are too high but by leaving a little power set the aircraft can be settled into ground effect and stopped at will once the power is taken off. The landing roll is short, and surprisingly noisy as the hook on the back end of the toothpick skid will catch in the ground causing an unexpected grating noise. Landings are done into wind.

CHAPTER SIX

Royal Aircraft Factory BE2c

Designed in 1912 by Geoffrey de Havilland, at the time working at the Royal Aircraft Factory in Farnborough, the BE2 was Britain's first ever military aeroplane, with 3,500 being built in total over the various derivatives. It was originally designed as a twin-bay biplane (i.e. it had two sets of struts between the wings on each side) with wing-warping for lateral control.

This might be a good point to try to explain the confusing number of different types built by the Royal Aircraft Factory. They were originally based on the configurations of aircraft available in the early years of the war: pusher engined, tractor engined and tail in front (like the Wright flyer) or behind.

- BE stood originally for Bleriot Experimental, meaning a tractor-engined configuration. It later came to mean British Experimental and effectively the standard design for most aircraft.
- FE stood for Farman Experimental, later Fighting Experimental, meaning a pusher-engined configuration.
- SE stood originally for Santos Experimental, thus the SE1 was originally a tail-first, or canard-designed, tractor-engined, but as the tail-first design was dropped (the SE2 was a standard tractor-engined biplane with its tail at the rear) the designation later became Scout Experimental.
- RE stood for Reconnaissance Experimental, mainly two-seaters.

As aircraft designs evolved these designations became meaningless and extremely confusing for modern people. Anyway, to try to explain why it is called a BE2c, it was the second design in the Bleriot Experimental range (i.e. tractor-engined and tail at the back) and the 'c' designation showed that was the third derivative of the BE2 range. It was actually a major redesign, first flying in May 1914 and owing much to research carried out by E. T. Busk, in that although it was still

The BE2c in all its glory. (Matthew Boddington)

a large twin-bay biplane, it had ailerons, whereas previous models of BE2 had wing-warping for lateral control. This made it even more stable and easy to fly – in fact it was the first aircraft of its kind to be able to be flown 'hands-off' – and in its early years it was a very effective, if very slow, reconnaissance aircraft. At the time stability was considered a good thing, allowing the aircraft to fly itself and the crew to devote all their time to observation and reconnaissance.

In 1915 aircraft had evolved to the point where they could be armed, and British pilots then discovered that stability was not a good thing. The BE2c and many other aircraft had very heavy controls with sluggish response, when what they needed was manoeuvrability so they would be able to get away from the notorious Fokker Eindeckers, with machine guns that fired through their propellers. During this period the BE2c pilots, and many others, became known as Fokker Fodder, but heroically they carried on doing their vital reconnaissance work despite the rising death toll.

So what is the story of the team's BE2c? Back in 1969, Charles Boddington, assisted by his brother David and a team of engineers, was given the seemingly impossible task of building and test-flying a BE2c replica in thirteen weeks for a proposed film to be called *Biggles Sweeps the Skies*. The only way to build an aircraft that quickly was to base it on an existing aircraft, so the BE2c was constructed using modified Tiger Moth parts, although it is difficult to see its heritage unless you look very closely. Not the least of the differences is the fact that the BE2c is a two-bay biplane with extra struts added to the wings to make it

The BE2c being relentlessly pursued by a Fokker. (Neil Woodhouse)

He shakes it off for the moment... (Carly Hodges)

... but of course there's no escape! (John Bilcliffe)

look more authentic. The Tiger Moth automatic slats on the top wings have also been removed.

Despite the ludicrous deadline, the aircraft was ready for shipment to Algeria, where the film was to be shot, on time. Sadly after all that work the film was scrapped, so the BE2c was shipped to America and sold by the film company who had funded the operation.

Charles Boddington was killed in a flying accident in 1970 and his creation, the BE2c, was wrecked when it spun into the ground in 1977 while flying to Old Rhinebeck Aerodrome in upper New York State – luckily the pilot survived. The wreckage ended up with a local Tiger Moth owner, who stored it in a barn, thinking maybe he might be able to use some of the parts one day.

Fast-forward to 2004 and Sywell-based Tiger Moth owner Chris Parker spotted the remains in the barn while visiting America and reported this back to Matthew Boddington, Charles's son, who was by then a licenced aircraft engineer repairing aircraft in a Sywell workshop next door to where his father had built the BE2c.

Matthew bought the remains and completely rebuilt it, incorporating various modifications that made the aircraft stronger and safer. It was finished in 2011 and Matthew started flying it with the team in 2013. In honour of its original build, it is known as the Biggles Biplane.

Another challenge that the team faced came at the very end of the rebuild when the aeroplane was rigged, to ensure the wings, struts and supporting wires are properly aligned and tensioned. While rigging any biplane is a complex and often infuriating procedure, the BE2 is a double-bay biplane with two pairs of interplane struts between the wings. There are no less than sixteen sets of flying and landing wires. Each needs to be accurately adjusted to allow the aeroplane to fly accurately.

Luckily, in 1918, a young Royal Naval Air Service aircraftsman named R. A. Randall kept a handwritten notebook throughout his training at Herne Bay in Kent. What happened to Randall is lost in time, but his notebook survives and in it, his personal notes on rigging the BE2. For Matthew and the team, it was like finding gold.

I have never flown the BE2c, although I have flown behind it many times and found it to be painfully slow, even compared to the SE5a replicas. I am therefore indebted to Francis Donaldson, chief engineer at the LAA, for allowing me to quote from a flight test report he wrote for the LAA magazine:

Probably the most noticeable feature of the Biggles biplane is the undercarriage, it has a custom-built wire braced wood and steel 'chassis' (as it was often referred to in the First World War era) with a bungee-sprung cross axle and long twin wooden skids, patterned after the undercarriage of the early BE types. The spoked wheels, naturally bereft of brakes, are built up on motorcycle rims with custom made extra-wide hubs

High-tail taxiing. (Steve Bridgewater/Awyr Aviation Communications)

A close-up showing the exhausts. (John Bilcliffe)

to cope with the side loads inevitable in an aircraft application. A substantial 'period looking' steerable ash tailskid at the rear is bungee-sprung and pylon-mounted, holding the tail higher off the ground than the more modern design of skid.

The engine in the Biggles Biplane is a 145 BHP Gipsy Major Mk 10 Mk 1, taken from a Beagle Terrier, but modified to run with cylinders uppermost. Unlike the original wet sump upright Gipsy engines, Matthew's upside down Gipsy Major engine preserves the Major's dry sump configuration, using three oil return pick-ups taken from what used to be the engine's top cover (now underneath). A separate cylindrical brass oil tank mounted transversely underneath the engine creates a strong visual feature, and thus exposed to the breeze, oil cooling is certainly not likely to be an issue.

A strong visual feature of the original BE2 range is its pair of parallel exhaust pipes. Often they are seen running back from each side of the engine, then climbing vertically, discharging each bank of the V8 over the upper wing. On the replica, the exhaust pipes reproduce the early 1914-era BE2s, sweeping downwards to exit under the fuselage. The exhaust pipe on the port side is functional but if you look closely in the pictures you'll see that the pipe on the starboard side is a dummy.

Handling-wise, The BE2's main feature is the heavy rudder and mild directional instability, both factors that came to light in the original tests and both, apparently, also shared with the full-sized BE2 recently built in New Zealand. Clearly the

An unbalanced rudder. (Steve Bridgewater/Awyr Aviation Communications)

Tiger Moth's characteristic fin and rudder shape, with aerodynamic horn balance, is not just for appearance sake as the BE clearly cries out for aerodynamic balance on the rudder to lighten the pedal forces and reduce the rudder's tendency to trail, sapping its effectiveness as a stabilising surface.

Aware of this instability I take care to keep the slip ball centred initially, then experiment with greater and greater slip angles to feel the BE out. Beyond a certain angle the yaw tries to increase, and needs positive foot force to get the ball back in the middle – not a characteristic you'd accept in a modern aeroplane, but not particularly unusual back in 1912. It's not difficult to control, provided that the rudder control circuit is intact, of course, but would be a problem if the rudder system were to come adrift. In this case, on the plus side, even if the yaw angle is allowed to increase to the maximum, the aeroplane remains controllable, cross-controlling on the stick to prevent a spiral dive developing.

In pitch, she is just positively statically stable, which is what we expect based on the flight test report, for we are right on the aft cg limit with my weight in the back seat and not a great deal of fuel in the front. At high speed the pitch control starts to feel a little sensitive, but in the normal 45-65 knot speed range she is predictable and easy to trim, the rush of wind over the airframe, and all those bracing wires, making speed easy to judge and the ASI almost superfluous.

After experimenting with the rudder, the BE2s 1930's style ailerons feel surprisingly light, typically Moth-ineffectual by modern standards, but perfectly adequate for the BE.

The power off stall occurs at just below 35 kts, and results in a shudder running through the airframe just before a mild g-break, wings remaining level, with the stick not quite on the back stop. Only by keeping the stick coming all the way to the stop can we force a wing to go down, the right wing gently falling away, instantly arrested as soon as the stick moves forward again.

I have spent many hours over the years behind Matthew in this aircraft and given the above I find it amazing he does such a good job of throwing it around the sky. I initially asked him whether the handling was as 'good' as a Tiger Moth or as bad as the Fokker (he had also flown a Dr1) and he answered: 'No it's not like a Tiger Moth, and that's bad enough. Yes it's probably as bad as the Fokker, however it has far more drag and its control/gust response is far worse! When Desmond Penrose flew it he reckoned it was the worst thing he had flown for being down low in gusty conditions, so just right for Airshows then!'

CHAPTER SEVEN

Royal Aircraft Factory SE5a Replica

The SE5 was designed and initially produced by the Royal Aircraft Factory at Farnborough in early 1917. It was almost immediately modified to become the SE5a by the fitting of a 200-hp Hispano-Suiza in place of the less reliable 150-hp Hispano-Suiza engine of the SE5. An improved, licence-built version of the Hispano-Suiza was later supplied by Wolseley Motors, known as the Wolseley Viper. It was one of the fastest and most nimble combat aircraft of the First World War and has been described as the Spitfire of that era. The SE5a and the Sopwith Camel, both introduced into service during 1917, helped the British gain air superiority during that year and remained in front-line service until the Armistice and beyond.

All SE5as in the team are 7/8th scale replicas built from the Canadian Replica Plans Co.'s plans, which were drawn up in the 1960s, with the first prototype flying in 1970.

The two longest-serving team members, Doug Gregory and Des Biggs, both built their own SE5as – G-SEVA and G-BMDB respectively – and flew them with the team from its inception in 1988 until 2012. Neither aircraft currently flies with the team.

Vic Lockwood's SE5a, G-CCBN, was built in America but was then sold to two brothers in Holland, who flew it on the Dutch register before Vic bought it in 2004. He joined the team in 2006. The aircraft represents one of the few that flew in American colours, Blue 19 of 25th Aero (or Pursuit) Squadron based at Toul. It is now owned by Arnd Schweisthal.

The first example to fly in Britain was G-BDWJ (representing F8010 of No. 85 Squadron RFC, believed to have been flown by Mick Mannock), which was built in 1978 by Mike Beach and previously flown with the team by Mark Smith. This aircraft now flies in the expert hands of ex-RAF Harrier display pilot Dave Linney, who started flying with the team in 2008, 'twenty-seven years after [his] third and last season displaying the Harrier'.

G-CCBN on the ground.

Climbing out.

Avoiding the flak. (Neil Woodhouse)

Dave doing his pre-flight check.

Flight-leader's pennants streaming.

The third current SE5a in the team is G-BUOD (painted to represent B595, a No. 56 Squadron aircraft in which Lieutenant Maurice Edmund Mealing MC achieved many of his victories). This was built by Mike Waldron in 1995 while he was living in Belgium. He offered it to the team in 2014 for someone to fly as he does not have a DA and I was dragged kicking and screaming out of retirement to fly it. It is now flown by Trevor Bailey.

After flying the Sopwith Triplane for fourteen years, flying Mike's SE5a was an untold luxury for me. With very little contortion it is possible to see down either side of the engine, so I could see far more of what was ahead of me than was possible in the Sopwith. There is even a reasonable view over the top of the cowling because the single (fake) Vickers gun is offset to the left (the Lewis gun is mounted on the top wing well out of the way, apart from occasionally banging your head on the mounting!).

Taxiing is simple; the tailskid is a flat piece of steel which presents no resistance to turning, so with stick forward, full rudder and a blast of power it will turn very quickly and easily. As if that wasn't enough, it has brakes! I'd never known such luxury; it was possible to taxi easily between parked aircraft and swing as tight as you wish onto the runway. Once lined up, with full power applied the tail comes up almost instantly, giving an unrestricted view of the runway ahead. As we always took off in a 'vic' formation, this meant that in my usual number three position, to the left of our leader Dave, I had an unrestricted view of both the other aircraft even if they moved up or down in the formation; this again was unheard of in the Sopwith.

Mike's SE5a ready to go.

Trevor trying to keep up with Dave.

The SE5a Flight lined up.

Emily managing to avoid banging her head.

A tight squeeze for Dave.

In flight the wonders increased – the controls actually worked! Being a late 1960s design it had modern ailerons, which were effective and reasonably powerful so you do not have to rely totally on the rudder. The stall is benign and the low-speed handling impeccable. What more could anyone ask of an aeroplane?

Well, there are a couple of minor problems that are common to most First World War types, and the worst is the lack of a crosswind capability. That flat steel tailskid that makes turning easy also allows the tail to swing easily in a crosswind. I once got back to my Croft Farm base, with its east–west runway, to find a south-easterly wind, which I calculated would mean a crosswind component of about 6 knots. This seemed acceptable and it seemed silly to divert to Staverton for such a small crosswind. My theory was that if I wheeled it on I could hold it straight with the rudder until I was in the lee of the hangars when the wind would drop off. It was a good theory, but sadly things didn't work out quite like that. As the aircraft slowed and the tail dropped, it suddenly veered sharply to the right, which meant I was now heading straight for the first hangar. I countered with full left rudder and a blast of power, and now I was heading straight for the hedge! Luckily after a few frantic seconds tap dancing on the brake and rudder pedals, I managed to get it back under control and swung off towards Mike's hangar. From then on I decided a 6-knot crosswind was the absolute limit for me in that aircraft.

The other problem? Well, having been used to having a large radial in front which produces huge amounts of heat both as hot air and from the hot oil tank above my feet, the SE has a smaller Continental flat four-cylinder engine, which, although it tends to run hot, does not provide much heat for the driver. Consequently the cross-country trip to Sywell for the pre-season practice in April or May always ended with me shivering in the cockpit no matter how many clothes I wore.

Dave Linney comments:

Although each example of the aeroplane sports a slightly different arrangement of cockpit controls and instruments the one common factor is its small dimensions meaning that even the more sylph-like pilots have little or no room to spare so cockpit management is of the essence. How to manipulate a map and any electronic (probably portable) navigation aids requires thought and cunning to say nothing of where to put weekend kit, spare oil, tie down pegs and ropes etc. The good thing though is that you 'put on' an SE5A and instantly feel part of it, not the case with all aeroplanes. In short the good old 'SE' is a sheer delight to both own and fly.

Recently one of the original SE5as that flew with the team, Mark Ordish's G-INNY, has returned. It is now based at Sywell and occasionally flown by Mark Johnson.

Little or no room to spare.

CHAPTER EIGHT

Junkers CL1

The original Junkers CL1 was a late war cantilever-wing monoplane design by Hugo Junkers as a ground-attack aircraft which had a metal-framed fuselage with corrugated aluminium skinning. Hugo Junkers had started building aircraft before the war and was a major proponent of both monoplane design and all-metal construction, including his famous corrugated skinning. The corrugated skinning became a Junkers feature, most famously in the Junkers Ju52 transport aircraft of the Second World War. As such, he was very much ahead of his time.

Junkers' first three 'J' series aircraft were all monoplanes, but its first success was with the biplane J4 (confusingly called the J1 by the military), which was ordered into production. After this Junkers went back to experimenting with the monoplane design.

Following a forced merger with the Fokker aircraft company, Junkers-Fokker produced the J9, designated D1 by the military, the world's first all-duralumin low-wing monoplane single seat fighter aircraft, and the J10 (renamed CL1), basically a two-seat ground attack derivative of the D1. Only fifty-one were built and as far as I can tell none were actually used in combat before the Armistice. They were designed to be a robust and fairly heavily armed aircraft, able to machine gun troops on the ground using the two forward-facing guns either side of the engine, while using the observer's rear-facing gun for protection.

The team's Junkers was a modification of John Day's 1960-designed Bowers Fly Baby, which he had built in 1987. This was to be used as a stop-gap when the Fokker that had flown with the team was sold so we would still have a German aircraft to dogfight with. It turned out to be such a useful aircraft that's it still flies with the team now, despite us having two Fokkers to dogfight.

John modified the turtle-deck to allow room for Hans, the observer/rear gunner, to sit in there with his machine gun (the usual remark from commentators is 'One of the people in that aircraft is a dummy, see if you can work out which it is!').

Two forward-firing machine guns and one in the rear for protection.

Of the two crew, one is a dummy. See if you can work out which!

Two machine guns and dummy cylinders.

To make it even more realistic, John had incorporated a mechanism linked to the rudder controls that makes Hans head turn from side to side as it taxis. He also built the dummy vertical cylinders for the engine and the two machine guns along the top of the cowling, as well as a new rudder and fin that more closely resembled the original.

John was very proud of the authentic-looking four-colour lozenge camouflage on the upper surface of the wing, although he said it took him ages to do. On original First World War German aircraft, the fabric was printed with the lozenge pattern in various colours and simply had to be fixed to the wing and doped, but of course John had to paint it, which meant making a stencil with the lozenge shapes repeated in a regular pattern then spraying one colour, moving the stencil once that colour was dry and spraying the next colour and so on. This was hugely time-consuming, but gave a very effective and authentic finish.

Despite all the modifications the aircraft remains a 1960-designed aircraft, with modern ailerons which are light and which actually work. It can be flown like a modern aircraft, using ailerons for roll and rudder for balance, unlike most aircraft in the team! The combination of fairly powerful ailerons and an effective rudder make it one of the better aircraft in the team for coping with wake turbulence. This makes it an ideal aircraft to give a new pilot an introduction to the team and the

Landing wires flapping in the breeze. (John Bilcliffe)

display. In fact, Mike Collett, who flies it often, commented: 'As an introduction or rite of passage into the GWDT you couldn't ask for anything better.' It can be enough of a problem coping with eight or nine other aircraft in close proximity, without having to worry about the strange handling characteristics of, say, the Sopwith or Fokker.

One minor point that can cause a moment's anguish if the pilot hasn't been briefed about it is the fact that the wires that are visible from the cockpit are, of course, the landing wires, so they take the weight of the wings (and are hence very taught on the ground) but do nothing in flight, and the sight of these once-taut wires flapping around in the breeze can be a bit disconcerting.

In mock combat it is fairly fast and manoeuvrable, which makes it a good adversary for the nimble SE5as. I have flown it in a display and after the Sopwith Triplane it really was a delight to fly. It can cope with hard runways due to its tail-wheel, and can even cope with stronger crosswinds than most of the team aircraft. The only point that can cause some concern on landing is there is no suspension apart from that supplied by the large balloon tyres, so if it is dropped on too hard it will bounce.

CHAPTER NINE

Nieuport 17

Built by John Day and Bob Gauld-Galliers using Walt Redfern's plans (which were themselves based on the contemporary Rozendaal drawings taken from a captured French machine), and completed in 1997, G-BWMJ is a replica Nieuport 17 and flew with the team from 1999 until 2011. The Nieuport is a sesquiplane, which in effect means it has one and a half wings. The one thing that sticks in my memory about this aircraft is how heavy the tail was; the undercarriage is slightly further forward than the Sopwith's, which means more of the weight is taken on the tailskid. The heavy tail does mean that if a swing starts to develop it needs to be stopped *immediately* before the pendulum effect takes over and makes it unstoppable, and the fact that the rudder is masked in the three-point attitude makes that very difficult. As Bob said: 'I have to say that when it's down the pilot becomes a passenger during the roll out!' The heavy tail also makes ground, handling a very definite two-man job just to lift the tail off the ground, and I recall straining my back many times to help heave this monster around with John or Bob.

When originally built the aircraft was painted to represent B3459 of No. 1 Squadron RFC, but after being used in the movie *Flyboys* it remains in its Escadrille Lafayette guise, with the fictional Flyboys markings replaced by the correct historical markings of Robert Soubiran of the Escadrille Lafayette. It is in those markings that she exists today as N1977 – N for Nieuport and 1,977th off the production line – with French roundels and a depiction of a Native American head on the side.

Another effect of this tail-heavy design, plus the fixed tailskid, is that manoeuvrability on the ground was never as good as the Sopwith's. I recall taxiing out to the runway once alongside Bob and I simply pushed the stick forward, gave a bootfull of rudder and the Sopwith swung easily onto the runway. After we landed Bob said: 'How is it that you can turn much tighter without brakes than I can *with* brakes?' That heavy tail took a lot of moving sideways!

An early picture of the Nieuport, with the Junkers in the background. (Sheila Truscott)

An airborne shot in the early days. (Sheila Truscott)

A later shot
in Escadrille
Lafayette colours.
(Steven Grey)

Although I never flew the Nieuport, I did fly alongside it on many occasions and, once in the air, it was a nimble beast, easily as capable of dogfighting as the Sopwith. This would be helped by the straight top wing, which means it lacks lateral stability, making it more manoeuvrable than its more stable contemporary (they were both delivered to front-line service from early 1916). Like all the First World War replicas, its most effective control is the rudder, which is much more useful in roll than the heavy and ineffective ailerons.

On the original aircraft the lower half-wing had a simple swivelling root fitting, which meant that the half-wing could be removed and replaced quickly and easily if damaged in the frequent ground-loops and landing accidents at the time; unfortunately, this often meant the lower wing could flutter, twist to form a *very* effective air brake, or even come off in flight (a problem which I believe was shared by the German Albatross sesquiplanes). Any of these problems could result in the loss of the aircraft and pilot, although I have seen one photo of a Nieuport which crash-landed with one lower wing missing! John and Bob sensibly followed Redfern's modifications and strengthened and braced the root system to make it much stronger and safer.

Bob gave me an article written by Bob Grimstead for *Aeroplane Monthly* in 2014, in which Bob assessed the handling and he commented about the lack of visibility common to most First World War aircraft. The top wing is just above the pilot's head, allowing upwards vision past the trailing edge and a limited band of visibility ahead between wing and fuselage. The narrow lower wing does give an excellent view downwards, at least when compared with other First World War types. With all these aircraft the view forward and downward in the landing attitude is never wonderful, but this is a reasonable compromise and, compared with any Triplane, excellent.

CHAPTER TEN

The Great War Display Team Today

With so much new blood and so many aircraft – at its peak we had ten – we could now do a more complex display. Originally the display had mainly consisted of formation fly-pasts, with maybe a loop from the Fokker (Nick's party piece, looping between 100 and 300 feet!) and a bit of a dogfight. Now we choreograph the routine, with different things happening at three levels and aircraft diving and climbing between the levels in hot pursuit of an enemy aircraft. We were, in fact, doing our best to show the crowd what it might have looked like during a real dogfight in 1917, the sky full of aircraft diving and wheeling around, each trying to get into a position from which he could shoot down an enemy.

The aim is to make it look as exciting as possible without putting anyone's life at risk. What looks from the ground like two aircraft narrowly missing each other is in fact done with a safe distance between the aircraft at all times. Given the paranoia since the Shoreham crash, safety has become paramount!

Over recent years we have added another dimension to the display thanks to our friends at Fireworks & FX Ltd, who provide very realistic-looking flak bursts as well as bomb explosions and strafing effects. We must be doing something right as during the 2018 season we did fifty shows – our busiest season ever.

We have also been asked to do various bits of filming, both for film and television. Members of the team flew in the film *Flyboys*, although most of it ended up on the cutting-room floor with the flying sequences being CGI. The Fokkers – and the Sopwith, bearing black crosses on its fuselage – appeared in the film *Wonder Woman*.

Over the years the team has appeared on TV many times, including Henry Allingham's funeral and the previously mentioned fly-past at the Thiepval monument. The most recent TV appearances were related to the centenary of the end of the First World War, including the BBC programme commemorating it, *RAF at 100*, fronted by the actor Ewan McGregor and his ex-RAF pilot brother Colin, as well as a programme featuring Sophie Raworth whose grandfather had flown in a BE2c and a feature about the centenary for *ITV News*.

(Steve
Bridgewater/
Awyr Aviation
Communications)

(John Bilcliffe)

(John Bilcliffe)

(Carly Hodges)

(Carly Hodges)

(Carly Hodges)

(Carly Hodges)

(Carly Hodges)

(Neil Woodhouse)

(Neil Woodhouse)

(Neil Woodhouse)

(Steve Bridgewater/Awyr Aviation Communications)

(Steve Bridgewater/Awyr Aviation Communications)

(Steve Bridgewater/Awyr Aviation Communications)

(Neil Woodhouse)

(Neil Woodhouse)

(Neil Woodhouse)

(Dave Page)

(Steve Bridgewater/Awyr Aviation Communications)

A Sopwith masquerading as a German. (Gordon Brander)

Ewan McGregor and Matthew getting ready to fly for the *RAF at 100* filming. (Freddie Claire)

Ewan and Matthew's BE2c climbing out over the bomb blasts. Mark is following, with Colin McGregor, in the Tiger Moth. (Freddie Claire)

Ewan seems to be enjoying his time in the BE2c! (Freddie Claire)

Ewan and Colin McGregor with Team Leader Gorden Brander – three Scots together! (Freddie Claire)

The team now has to have a leader; organising this many aircraft, which operate from bases all over the southern half of England to do so many shows each year, doesn't just happen by chance. The promotion of the team and contacting display organisers, to say nothing of the mountain of paperwork required for each aircraft and pilot for each show, by the post-Shoreham regulations is almost a full-time job. At the time of writing, and for many years, the leader has been Gordon Brander, the current owner and pilot of the Sopwith, with IT help from the author. The years 2014 to 2018 were of course particularly busy, with every major show wanting to remember the centenary of the First World War. Being painfully slow and with limited range, it is difficult to do more than one show per day unless they are very close together, so we have had to turn down some shows on logistical grounds. Gordon, being a Scot, would love to do a show north of the border, but it simply isn't feasible.

Some of our logistical problems would simply not occur with most modern pilots. For instance, these aircraft were designed before runways, let alone hard runways, were invented. We have to land on grass, especially those aircraft with tail skids instead of tail wheels. The skid is the brake as well as the steering – it has to bite into the grass or else it would be like landing on ice – and we have little or no crosswind capability. Originally these aircraft would have operated from a large grass field so they could land directly into wind, whatever the wind direction. Very few current British airfields are large grass fields with the option of landing in any direction, and that ignores the attitude of the airfield management who, in some cases, are not prepared to allow aircraft to land anywhere except on the designated runways on health and safety grounds. Angling off the runway to reduce the cross-wing component might result in you being banned for life. Life can be tricky enough in these aircraft without having to put up with the stupidity of jobsworths who can't fly and don't care how much trouble they cause as long as we obey the rules.

The designers of these aircraft didn't care too much about pilot safety and comfort, and the Triplanes in particular have very restricted visibility. Trying to land in the classic three-point attitude means you can't see anything forward or downwards, so you have to aim for where you last saw the runway and hope nobody has moved it. On the ground, obstructions ahead are invisible. For these reasons you will notice that all three Triplanes do wheeler landings whenever possible – with the tail up, you have at least some idea of where you are going and what is ahead. You might also notice that Alex, in Bruce's Fokker, taxis while sitting on the seat-back to give himself some idea where he is going, although I have no idea how he does it and maintains control. The other two manage with what they can see between the fuselage and the mid wing, which is not very much and nothing at all dead ahead.

A Sopwith landing and about to get bounced.

Bruce's Fokker landing.

Peter's Fokker landing.

Alex taxiing.

The team has now been around for thirty years and has evolved beyond recognition from what it was at the start. What will the future bring? Well, I hope it will carry on for many years to come. What we do is unique in the UK, with so many aeroplanes wheeling and diving in such close proximity, and it has proved popular at airshows over the years – especially recently, with the First World War centenary – and I would like to think it will carry on doing so. There are, of course, fewer pilots who have experience of this kind of aircraft but they are not particularly difficult to fly, just different, and with training most pilots could master them. All they need is the desire!

Here's to the next thirty years!